QUEER EYE

FIND THE FAB FIVE

QUEER EYE

FIND THE FAB FIVE

A TOTALLY FIERCE SEEK-AND-FIND

LAUREN EMILY WHALEN

ILLUSTRATED BY
MICHELLE BARON

Running Press
PHILADELPHIA

Running Press
Hachette Book Group
1290 Avenue of the Americas, New York, NY 10104
www.runningpress.com
@Running_Press

Printed in China

First Edition: October 2023

Published by Running Press, an imprint of Perseus Books, LLC, a subsidiary of Hachette Book Group, Inc. The Running Press name and logo are trademarks of the Hachette Book Group.

The Hachette Speakers Bureau provides a wide range of authors for speaking events. To find out more, go to www.hachettespeakersbureau.com or email HachetteSpeakers@hbgusa.com.

Running Press books may be purchased in bulk for business, educational, or promotional use. For more information, please contact your local bookseller or the Hachette Book Group Special Markets Department at Special.Markets@hbgusa.com.

The publisher is not responsible for websites (or their content) that are not owned by the publisher.

Print book cover and interior design by Jenna McBride
Print book cover and interior illustrations by Michelle Baron

Library of Congress Control Number: 2022949629

ISBNs: 978-0-7624-8268-9 (hardcover), 978-0-7624-8269-6 (ebook), 978-0-7624-8649-6 (ebook), 978-0-7624-8652-6 (ebook)

APS

10 9 8 7 6 5 4 3 2 1

CONTENTS

INTRODUCTION

THE FAB FIVE are all about self-love, confidence, acceptance, and helping others to discover the best version of themselves. They also . . . know how to have fun! Come along with Tan, Antoni, Jonathan, Karamo, and Bobby on their day-to-day adventures as they work their magic spreading love and joy everywhere they go.

On the following pages are fifteen scenes where you'll find the Fab Five. You might catch Tan rummaging through the latest threads at the thrift shop, Bobby reinventing someone's space, or even Antoni cooking up a new trendy meal. But they need your help! In each location, you'll need to find each member of the Fab Five—plus Antoni's adorable pooch, Neon—as well as other important items and accessories. Head to the checklists at the back of the book to see how many items you can find (pages 32–33), then check out the answer key starting on page 34 to see how you did. Good luck, queen!

FUN AND FABULOUS THRIFTING

Hello, luv! I'm not the only one who loves thrift shops. The entire Fab Five likes nothing more than finding gorgeous looks and items to brighten up our style and spaces—and thrifting is good for the environment, too. But now I'm having trouble finding my friends as well as the best bargains to help our hero feel fabulous. Can you assist? And always remember to French tuck it!

COOKING UP ADVENTURE

Food is a form of love. I'm always happiest at my favorite restaurants— and when the Fab Five come along, a good night is made even better! I want to craft the most delicious experience possible for whomever I am hosting, but I'm having trouble keeping track of everyone. Your mission is to find Karamo, Jonathan, Tan, Bobby, and me before the first course hits the table!

LOOK YOUR FIERCEST

Hey, queen! Ready to indulge in the most gorgeous self-care? I can't wait to do your hair and make you the absolute best version of your fantastic self. We can also get massages, manicures, makeup, whatever you want—it's your special day! My besties—the Fab Five—are also getting pampered. Let's find them together and have a dance party while we do it!

SALON + WELLNESS CENTER

BUILDING UP THE BEST

Hey, y'all! Welcome to one of my favorite places—the construction site is where all the magic happens. We've got our hard hats on and are ready to dive into projects that will make your home feel like home! Of course, the Fab Five is all over the place, and I need your help on a special task—don't forget to look absolutely everywhere, because one of them *might* be sleeping on the job!

LET'S GET PHYSICAL

Working out is good for your body and soul, and it's way more fun with friends! A boxing match, a cardio dance class, or even aerial arts—the ways to "get physical" are endless here. Don your brightest workout clothes and join me and the QE crew as we find the best ways to get our sweat on. We can even get our steps in by finding the missing items!

JUICE BAR

BEAUTIFUL BOUTIQUE

This fantastic shop is ours for the day! I'm so excited to dress you up, whether you're looking for a casual style or a fabulous formal for a special occasion—or both! Let's take a look around and see what clothes stand out to us, then head to the dressing room to put together the trendiest looks. In the meantime, we'll seek out the rest of the Fab Five—they're around here somewhere!

TOO MANY COOKS?

There are never too many cooks in the kitchen, as far as I'm concerned! Of course, I'm the only one who's actually doing any work—everyone else is finding snacks, hiding among the pots and pans, or trying to eat all the food. Sigh. And the pup is around here somewhere—c'mere, boy! Can you help me find everyone and everything before the dinner bell rings?

COOKIES

ARF! ARF!

Oh em gee, I absolutely *adore* these precious pooches! Look at them strutting around the park in their gorgeous element—I think I'll strut along with them. While we squee at our favorites and see if they'll let us style them, we'll take a stroll around and show off our own 'dos! Where is that Fab Five of mine? Has Antoni adopted every dog in the park yet?

NO PLACE LIKE HOME

Do you love our loft as much as we do? No matter where the Fab Five goes, I make sure our space is the loveliest, most comfortable place for us to hang out, spill tea, and celebrate our heroes. There are places for "me time" as well as spots to gather, so finding my pals can be quite the challenge. Don't forget to explore every nook and cranny on your search!

LET'S JAM!

Pump it up! I love a good record, and this vintage record store is one of the best. Albums make great conversation starters and there are tons of artists to choose from. You might even find some old instruments we can play together (in my case, very badly!). Plus, there's every type of music under the sun. Pick your favorite tunes and come join the Fab Five!

WERK IT!

There's no better place to show off your sassiest look than the runway! All sizes and shapes are beautiful, so don't be afraid to roll up with full confidence so you can feel your absolute best. The Fab Five and I will even walk with you (in our own best outfits). Time to strut!

FARM TO FABULOUS

The farmers' market is my favorite place! So many ingredients for beautiful dishes and lots of ways to share love through recipes. Here you can find plants, candles, yummy free samples, and sometimes even live entertainment. And, of course, my pup is paws-itively content, especially when the vendors give him treats. There are also countless places for goodies to hide—help me find the Fab Five and let's keep an eye out!

MASQUERADE ON PARADE

Yaassss, I love a costume party! We have masks! We have fabulous outfit realness! We have a DJ and dancing! Costumes allow you to be creative, show other sides of your personality, and are a great way to connect with new people and find out things about your friends. Let's track down the rest of the QE dream team—we're all in disguise, but I love a challenge, don't you? Don't forget to sashay, sashay, sashay!

FURNISH YOUR LIFE

This furniture store has so many possibilities for your home's "make-better"! Let's take our time, try out *everything* that looks comfortable, and pick out the pieces you like best. Don't forget to research, research, research. Look online for designs you like and how to incorporate them into your living space. Find items that match your style but also work with the room. I hope you don't mind—I brought the Fab Five along to give us their opinions, but, of course, they've already scattered. Oh no, someone's swinging from a chandelier! Behave, y'all!

MARCH WITH PRIDE

Celebrating who you are is the most important act of all! The Fab Five loves a Pride parade—Pride commemorates LGBTQ identity and history, and more than that, it's always a rockin' good time. Come join us on the Fab Five float, dance your cares away, and make new friends amid the rainbows. No matter what community you fit in, show off what makes you special. Celebrate Pride!

CHECKLISTS

When you're done finding the Fab Five (and Neon!), see if you can find these other items:

FUN AND FABULOUS THRIFTING

- ☐ Antique frame
- ☐ Vintage vest
- ☐ Graphic tee
- ☐ Dog sculpture
- ☐ Sewing machine
- ☐ Vase

COOKING UP ADVENTURE

- ☐ Toaster
- ☐ 7 menus
- ☐ Bow tie
- ☐ Food processer
- ☐ Carving knife
- ☐ Sliced fruit

LOOK YOUR FIERCEST

- ☐ Makeup brushes
- ☐ Slippers
- ☐ Sleeping eye masks
- ☐ Rainbow towel
- ☐ Robe
- ☐ Fashion magazine
- ☐ Hair scissors
- ☐ Broom
- ☐ Nail polish
- ☐ Nail clipper

BUILDING UP THE BEST

- ☐ 2 hammers
- ☐ 8 pink hard hats
- ☐ Pride construction vest
- ☐ 5 paint cans
- ☐ Design plans
- ☐ Measuring tape

LET'S GET PHYSICAL

- ☐ Rack of barbells
- ☐ Water bottle
- ☐ Bounce ball
- ☐ Purple kettlebell
- ☐ Rowing machine

BEAUTIFUL BOUTIQUE

- ☐ Bandana
- ☐ Pink flower dress
- ☐ Cowboy boots
- ☐ Sunglasses
- ☐ Tie

TOO MANY COOKS?

- ☐ Kitchen towel
- ☐ Electric mixer
- ☐ Cookie jar
- ☐ Ice cream tub
- ☐ Bowl of lemons
- ☐ Wine bottle
- ☐ Spatula
- ☐ Dog bowls

ARF! ARF!

- ☐ Lost basketball
- ☐ Ice cream cone
- ☐ Picnic basket
- ☐ Poodle
- ☐ Playground rings
- ☐ Pizza
- ☐ Guitar
- ☐ Kettlebell

NO PLACE LIKE HOME

- ☐ Facemask
- ☐ Dog bed
- ☐ Yoga mat
- ☐ Book
- ☐ Hair gel
- ☐ Laptop
- ☐ Chess

LET'S JAM!

- ☐ Drum
- ☐ Violin
- ☐ Recorder
- ☐ Golden record player
- ☐ Microphone
- ☐ Trophy

WERK IT!

- ☐ Hair styling tools
- ☐ Red heels
- ☐ Reporter's notebook
- ☐ Ironing board
- ☐ 2 sewing machines
- ☐ Cheerleaders
- ☐ Giraffe costume

FARM TO FABULOUS

- ☐ Sunhat
- ☐ Tote bag
- ☐ Pup's lost leash
- ☐ Balloons
- ☐ 2 chalkboards
- ☐ Bubbles
- ☐ Hopscotch

MASQUERADE ON PARADE

- ☐ Jester mask
- ☐ Cape
- ☐ Bunny ears
- ☐ Cupcake
- ☐ Cake
- ☐ Grapes
- ☐ Punchbowl
- ☐ Pitchfork

FURNISH YOUR LIFE

- ☐ Vase
- ☐ Candles
- ☐ Lightbulb
- ☐ Picture frames
- ☐ Pride flag
- ☐ Purple hat
- ☐ Trampoline

MARCH WITH PRIDE

- ☐ Sunglasses
- ☐ "Love is love" sign
- ☐ Megaphone
- ☐ Crop tops
- ☐ Bicycle
- ☐ Unicorn ears
- ☐ Peace sign

KEY

FUN AND FABULOUS THRIFTING

COOKING UP ADVENTURE

LOOK YOUR FIERCEST

BUILDING UP THE BEST

LET'S GET PHYSICAL

BEAUTIFUL BOUTIQUE

TOO MANY COOKS?

ARF! ARF!

NO PLACE LIKE HOME

LET'S JAM!

WERK IT!

FARM TO FABULOUS

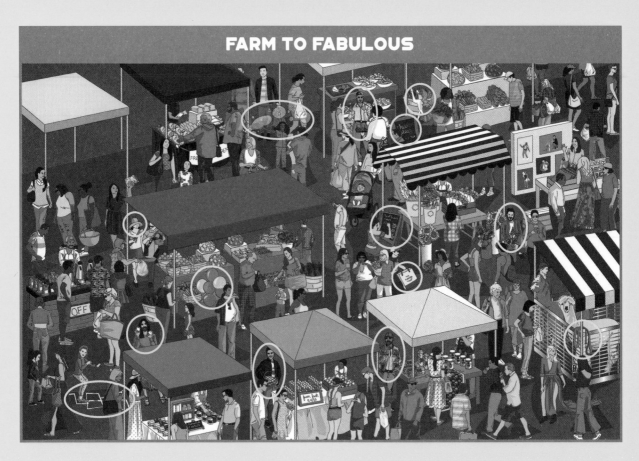

MASQUERADE ON PARADE

FURNISH YOUR LIFE

MARCH WITH PRIDE